Israel at War

Israel at War

What the Bible Says About Today's Crisis

Rev. Barbara M. Schobl-Legee

Legee Publishing, LLC

Legee Publishing LLC
P. O. Box 365
Waverly, FL 33877

Copyright © 2024 by Legee Publishing

All rights reserved.

No part of this publication may be reproduced, distributed, or transmitted in any form or by any means, including photocopying, recording, or other electronic or mechanical methods, without the prior, written permission of the publisher, except as allowed by U. S. copyright law. For permission requests, contact Legee Publishing, P.O. Box 365, Waverly, FL 33877, or LegeePublishing@gmail.com

All quoted Scripture is the King James Version (KJV) unless otherwise noted.

Due to the changing nature of the Internet, if there are any web addresses, links, or URLs included in this manuscript, these may have been altered and may no longer be accessible.

ISBNs:

978-1-966711-31-5 Kindle

978-1-966711-32-2 Paperback

978-1-966711-33-9 PDF

978-1-966711-33-9 EPUB

978-1-966711-34-6 Try Before You Buy

About the Book

The first edition was done as a "Quick and Dirty" version to get it out so others could have a quick read about what was going on in Israel.

This Second Edition has the background story, going back to Genesis and Creation. It covers the history of God's people through September 18, 2024.

As one young lady told me, "I knew there was something going on to cause that (War in Israel)."

I hope you enjoy the full story of God's love for His people and the discipline He gives to correct them.

Contents

Israel is Attacked!	1
In The Beginning,	3
Canaan Land and the Books of Joshua and Judges	13
Samuel	21
Chronicles	23
Baal Worship in Jerusalem	25
Baal Worship in Samaria	29
Other Gods	33
The Book of Amos	37
The Book of Hosea	41
The Book of Zephaniah	47
The Book of Ezekiel	53
The Book of Isaiah	57
The Book of Malachi	61
Surrounded by their enemies	65
The End Times	67
The Book of Revelation	71

Now You Know	79
Post Script:	81
Other Books by the Author	85
About the Author	87

Israel is Attacked!

October 7, 2023— Concert attendees were attacked at the edge of the Gaza Strip by Hamas. They heard the rockets around 6:30 a.m. By 7:00 a.m., they were running as Gaza militants fired at them. At least 260 bodies would later be found at the festival site. Some attendees were taken hostage.[1]

Concertgoers had been dancing under a giant statue of Buddha. People had come there "to hear music, to do love; they wanted to live," one survivor told.[2]

It is almost 50 years to the day since the last time Israel was officially at war in what is known as the Yom Kippur War in 1973, when she was attacked by Egypt, Syria, and others. But this is a different kind of war.

Fifty years is significant—it indicates a Jubilee year. Seven cycles of seven years in each cycle. The following year is the Jubilee.

What was wrong with that? Was God angry? Why did He allow that to happen? I've been told any number of times, "God does not

---

1. https://www.cnn.com/2023/10/07/middleeast/israel-gaza-fighting-hamas-attack-music-festival-intl-hnk/index.html

2. https://www.nbcnews.com/news/world/israel-music-festival-massacre-grounds-rcna120148

get angry;" or, "God does not want retribution;" or, "God would not do that!"

Let's start with the history of God's people.

In The Beginning,

God created the Heavens and the Earth (Genesis 1:1).
In Genesis 1:26-27, we read: *"Then God said, 'Let Us make man in Our image, according to Our likeness; let them have dominion over the fish of the sea, over the birds of the air, and over the cattle, over all the Earth and over every creeping thing that creeps on the Earth'. 27) So God created man in His own image; in the image of God He created him; male and female He created them* (Genesis 1:26-27). Notice the plural, "Us," in verse 26.

This was the beginning of God's relationship with His children. He had created them; "fathered" them.

Genesis 2 expands on this creation:

God planted a garden in Eden and put the man there to tend the garden and keep it. (Genesis 2:8, 15). There was no woman at that time. God made every tree that is pleasant to look at and good for food. There were also two trees in the middle of the Garden: The Tree of Life and the Tree of the Knowledge of Good and Evil. God told Adam in Genesis 2:16-17 And the LORD God commanded the man, saying, Of every tree of the garden thou mayest freely eat: 17) But of the tree of the knowledge of good and evil, thou shalt not eat of it: for in the day that thou eatest thereof thou shalt surely die. This word, translated into *die*, was the Hebrew word *muth*. But an interesting thing is noted: the word is repeated in the manuscripts: *muth muth. Die die*—the second death—separation from God.

There was a river to water the Garden, which parted and became four rivers. So, we see the four rivers flowed together and became one: the Euphrates, which flows into the Persian Gulf.

God then made woman. He caused a deep sleep to fall on Adam. While he was sleeping, God took one of his ribs and then closed up Adam. Then God made the rib into a woman and, when Adam had awakened, brought the woman to him. They were naked and not ashamed.

In the Garden, there was a serpent, more cunning than any beast of the field (Genesis 3:1). He came to Eve and asked, "Has God indeed said, 'You shall not eat of every tree of the garden?'"

That is one way Satan lures us into sin—he casts doubt on God's word.

While Adam had told Eve they could eat of any tree in the Garden but the Tree of the Knowledge of Good and Evil, Eve adds something else to that statement when she answers the serpent: "We may eat the fruit of the trees of the garden; but the fruit of the tree which is in the middle of the garden, God has said, 'You shall not eat it, **nor shall you touch it,** lest you die.'"

Although God had not recorded the part about touching it, it still represents another way Satan lures us into sin: he has us touch the forbidden fruit. After all, if it doesn't hurt when you touch it, it should be OK, right?

The serpent told her, "You will not surely die." This word, again, is *muth*. But it is only used once. Satan did not mention the second death. This was the first death. And He was right. They did not physically die. However, when they got through eating, they knew they were naked, and they became ashamed and made fig leaves for coverings for their bodies. They would have to replace those fig leaves every day or so because they would rot and shrink, leaving them naked again.

God found them in the Garden. They were hiding from Him because they were ashamed. But, they became separated from God—that second death. God kicked them out of the Garden of Eden, but not before God made animal skin tunics (Genesis 3:21) for them—the first sacrifice for man's sin. An animal had to die because man sinned. That poor animal had done nothing wrong, but it was the "scapegoat" and took Adam and Eve's sins upon itself and was sacrificed.

Then we come to Cain and Abel. Cain grew fruit, and Abel raised sheep. Cain brought the first fruits for a sacrifice, and Abel brought the firstborn of his flock. God respected Abel's offering but did not respect Cain's offering. Cain became angry. He was so angry that he killed Abel. God sentenced him to be a fugitive and a vagabond, with the Earth not yielding to him. Because Cain was worried someone might kill him (Heaven forbid that someone should do to him what he did to his own brother!), God set a mark on him so no one would kill him. Then Cain "went out from the presence of the Lord..." (Genesis 4:3-16)—that separation from God again.

As man multiplied on the Earth, they became more wicked in the sight of the Lord, and He was sorry He had made man. He vowed to destroy man (Genesis 6:5-7).

Genesis 6:8 *But Noah found grace in the eyes of the Lord.*

Noah built an ark. There were no boats back then. And the Ark was huge! God told Noah it was going to rain. There was no rain back then:

Genesis 2:5-6 *And every plant of the field before it was in the Earth, and every herb of the field before it grew: for the LORD God had not caused it to rain upon the earth, and there was not a man to till the ground. 6) But there went up a mist from the Earth, and watered the whole face of the ground.*

I can only imagine Noah's questions

"Lord, what's an ark?"

"Lord, what's rain?"[1]

Scientists believe there were periods in our planet's past when there might have been an ice layer around the Earth. This is known as "Snowball Earth." Geological and atmospheric records reveal signs of ancient glaciation, especially from the era known as "Snowball Earth." These signs include preserved gases within ice core samples, distinct rock formations such as tillites and erratics, and shifts in the composition of Earth's atmosphere over time.

The Flood destroyed all the people except Noah and his family (and apparently a few others in certain parts of the world – Moses would later encounter the descendants of the Nephilim).

It wasn't too long before the Tower of Babel happened. People got together and decided to build a tower to Heaven. They did that in the "Land of Shinar." This is where a woman, called Wickedness, would later be put in a basket, delivered to the "Land of Shinar," and set on a base there (Zechariah 5:5-11). But that's another story.

The people of Babel wanted to "make a name for" themselves (Genesis 11:4). Because all the people spoke one language, this was possible. So, God said, "Let Us (notice the plural—just as in Genesis 1:26) go down there and confuse their speech" (Genesis 11:7). A fitting punishment. At least God did not kill anyone. The punishment kept the people from scheming against Him for a little while.

---

1. Credit to Bill Cosby

The next time we see God's destruction is at Sodom and Gomorrah. Two evil cities! By Genesis 14, Abraham's brother, Lot, was living in Sodom. He was taken captive in a battle, and he later returned. When God was ready to destroy those cities, Abraham interceded for Sodom. After all, his brother was there! Abraham convinced God that if there were as few as ten righteous people there, God would not destroy it. Well, we all know how well that went!

Two angels went to Lot's house to warn him about the destruction. They did not want to stay in Lot's house but "in the open square." Lot finally convinced them to stay inside his house. That evening, the men of Sodom—both old and young—came and demanded the "men" (angels) so they could "know them carnally" (Genesis 19:2-5).

The angels convinced Lot they would destroy the city and everyone in it. So, Lot and his family left. The angels told them not to look back. Lot's wife did look back, and her pillar of salt is still in the land. My father went to the Middle East and saw the pillar of salt. He took a picture of it. It looked like a small human figure, wrapped in a cloak that covered its face. My father said the tour guide told them they were no longer allowed to pick pieces off the pillar, but even so, they could see it was "complete." The tour guide said that when someone picked a piece of the pillar, they would find it had grown back the next day. Interesting! Wonder how true it was? Why would they stop people from getting small pieces if it were true?

We don't know who those people were in Sodom and Gomorrah. Were they once God's people? After all, He made the first man, and everyone descended from them. These people were SO evil that God destroyed two entire cities. No mercy! According to The Comets of God by Dr. Jeffrey Goodman, the cities were destroyed by comets. Very possible.

Here is another thought for you: The sin the men of Sodom wanted to commit against the Angels of the Lord is a sin that is prevalent in the world today. Sodomy. Man lying with man. God is the same yesterday, today, and forever (Hebrews 13:8). He does not change (Malachi 3:6).

Eventually, the Hebrew people ended up in Egypt, saved from a famine by Joseph, who was "sold into slavery" by his brothers. All was well for approximately 400 years until a Pharaoh arose who did not know who Joseph was (Exodus 1:8). He saw the Hebrews were more numerous than the people of Egypt, and he began to "deal shrewdly with them" (Exodus 1:10), The Egyptians set taskmasters over the Hebrews "to afflict them with their burdens" (Exodus 1:11).

All this was NOT a punishment for the Hebrew children. This was part of God's plan to make them uncomfortable where they were, so they would leave Egypt and go to the Promised Land: Canaan. God wanted them in one place so they could become a nation. They had wandered as nomads before, but they needed to learn how to become a national group of people. Also, by being in slavery, they would learn to become a nation without becoming a threat to other nations. God raised up Moses to lead them. How long after the afflictions began? Moses was born after the afflictions started, and the Egyptians were killing the male babies when they were born. Moses was rescued and grew up in Pharaoh's household. Moses was 40 years old when he killed the Egyptian (Acts 7:23-24). Forty years later, Moses spoke with a burning bush that was not consumed. The voice from the bush told him to go back to Egypt and bring His (God's) people out of Egypt and into "the land which I swore to give to Abraham, Isaac, and Jacob." Moses, at first, had all kinds of excuses for not going. God became angry with Moses (Exodus 4:14). Moses relented, and he and Aaron headed to Egypt. Moses, by then, was 80 years old (Exodus 7:7).

After ten plagues, Moses, with God's guidance, led the Hebrew people out of Egypt. Along the way, they grumbled and griped, asking, "Why have you taken us away to die in the wilderness? It would have been better for us to serve the Egyptians than that we should die in the wilderness" (Exodus 14:11-12). Things got a little better. God provided sweet water for them, commanding Moses to strike the rock. He provided manna from Heaven for them. When they got tired of the manna, God provided quail.

On the way to Canaan, Moses went up on Mount Sinai to meet with God. While on Mount Sinai, God gave Moses the Ten Commandments, the Law of the Altar, the Law Concerning Servants, the Law Concerning Violence, Animal Control Laws, Responsibility for Property, Moral and Ceremonial Principles, Justice for All, the Law of Sabbaths, and a commandment for Three Annual Feasts (Unleavened Bread, Feast of Harvest, and the Feast of Ingathering). Moses went down to the people and told them what God had said. Then, he went back up the mountain with Joshua. God gave him the tablets with the Ten Commandments on them. They were there for 40 days and nights. He told Moses about the Offerings for the Sanctuary, the Ark of the Testimony they would build, the Table for the Showbread, Gold Lampstand, Tabernacle, Altar of Burnt Offering, Court of the Tabernacle, Care of the Lampstand, Garments for the Priesthood, Ephod, and the breastplate and other Priestly Garments. He also spoke to Moses about consecrating Aaron and his sons, the Daily Offerings, Altar of Incense, Bronze Laver, Holy Anointing Oil, Incense, artisans for building the Tabernacle, and the Sabbath Law.

All was well until Moses came off the mountain. Aaron had been confronted by the people, who said they didn't know what had happened to Moses. Aaron's response? Give me all your gold. And he made a golden calf. The people responded, "This is your god, O Israel, that brought you out of the land of Egypt!" Whoa! Breaking Commandment #1! Aaron had the audacity to build an altar and place it before the golden calf.

God told Moses what was going on, and neither of them was very happy about it. God wanted to destroy them right then (Exodus 32:10). Moses pleaded with God, and God did not destroy the people. But when Moses saw the golden calf and the people dancing, Moses broke the Ten Commandments. He threw the tablets and broke them at the foot of the mountain. Aaron's excuse? "You know the people, that they are set on evil. They told me to make gods to go before us. I took their gold and threw it in the fire, and this calf jumped out!" (Thou shalt not bear false witness!)

Moses called God's people to him and had them take their swords and kill their brothers, their companions, and their neighbors. About 3,000 people died that day. All this at God's command.

It would only be the beginning!

New tablets were made, and the covenant was renewed.

In Numbers 21:4-9, God made them victorious in battle against the Canaanites, and then they started grumbling again. "Why have you brought us up out of Egypt to die in the wilderness? For there is no food, no water, and our soul loathes this worthless bread (manna)." So, the Lord sent fiery serpents among the people, and they bit the people, and many of the people of Israel died. In response, God told Moses to make a bronze serpent and put it on a pole for the people to see. If a snake bit someone, they could look at the bronze serpent and be saved.

Later, the Israelites shifted their worship to Baal of Peor (Numbers 25:1-9). Despite Balaam's attempts to curse them, God intervened. This incident was part of a recurring pattern, beginning with the

Exodus, where God's acts of salvation were met with complaints and apostasy.

At Mount Peor in Moab, the Israelite men were drawn to Moabite women and participated in their religious festivals. Baal of Peor, a chief deity of the Moabites, Midianites, and Ammonites, was worshiped. These feasts involved sacrificial meals, which, in the ancient world, were acts of worship to the deity to whom the meal was dedicated (Numbers 25:2).

The Israelites who attended these feasts not only ate the sacrificial meals but also worshiped the Moabite gods, leading to severe consequences (Numbers 25:4). The punishment for worshiping other gods was death, with the offenders' bodies left exposed as a warning, a practice also employed by the Assyrians.

In Deuteronomy 4:44-49, Moses sets the stage for his second speech, recounting Israel's journey to the east side of the Jordan. The speech begins with a summary of the covenant obligations (chapters 5-11) and emphasizes the importance of obedience for enjoying covenant blessings. The latter part (Deuteronomy 12:1-26:19) details specific laws, blending civil, ceremonial, and moral instructions.

Moses' speech primarily aimed to motivate the Israelites to adhere to their covenant obligations upon entering the Promised Land (highlighted in chapters 6-11). The prohibition in Deuteronomy 5:8-9 underscores that bowing to idols equated to worshiping deities represented by those images, a common practice in the ancient Near East.

In Egypt, gods were believed to inhabit their statues, which were treated as the god's body. At the same time, in Mesopotamia, a ritual known as "opening the mouth" transformed a crafted image into the deity's presence. Conversely, Israel's worship was devoid of images, with Deuteronomy 5:8-9 explicitly banning the creation of any likeness, including that of the God of Israel.

Magic permeated ancient societies and was used to foretell the future, influence events, and counteract evil. However, as stated in Deuteronomy 18:10-11, Israel's law forbade all forms of magic and divination, viewing them as abominations practiced by the Canaanites. Legitimate methods of seeking God's will included the Urim and Thummim, the ephod, lots, and dreams (1 Samuel 14:41; 23:9-12; 28:6).

Pagan divination practices, such as teratoscopy—interpreting birth anomalies—were explicitly banned in Israel (Deuteronomy 18:10). These practices, considered perverse forms of revealing divine secrets, were strictly prohibited, reinforcing the distinction between trusting in God and relying on human wisdom and signs.

Deuteronomy 32:16-18 *They provoked him to jealousy with strange gods, with abominations provoked they him to anger. 17) They sacrificed unto devils, not to God; to gods whom they knew not, to new gods that came newly up, whom your fathers feared not. 18) Of the Rock that begat thee thou art unmindful, and hast forgotten God that formed thee.*

Notice here that the strange gods are called "devils."

Canaan Land and the Books of Joshua and Judges

God had told the Israelites to kill all the people and animals of the land of Canaan when they went in to take the land. However, some Israelite conquests involved peaceful assimilation of native peoples, such as with the Gibeonites (Joshua 9). Such assimilation posed the risk of blending the Israelite faith with Canaan's religious beliefs and practices. The Canaanites worshiped many deities, including El, the great sky god, and his consort, Asherah. By the time of the conquest, worship of El had mainly been replaced by the worship of Baal, a warrior storm god.

Who was Asherah? In Canaan, she was called Astarte. In Sumeria, she was known as Inanna. In Assyria, Babylon, she was called Ishtar. To the Romans, she was Venus. To the Greeks, Aphrodite. She was a temptress. She was the patron goddess of the tavern, associated with drinking beer. In the Bible, she is called Ashteroth, Ashtaroth, Ashtereth, Asherah, and Astaroth. The people used Asherah (Asherim) poles, named after the goddess Asherah, which were totem poles or trees, to worship her. Trees were sometimes planted in "groves" to worship her. A grave could also consist of several Asherah (Asherim) poles. Much of Israel's religious history centers around the conflict between the worshipers of the one God of the Exodus and those who followed the Canaanite deities.

Joshua 15:63 says, *"[T]he Jebusites... the children of Judah could not drive them out; but the Jebusites dwell with the children of Judah at Jerusalem to this day."*

In the land of Ephraim, Joshua 16:10 states, *"And they did not drive out the Canaanites who dwelt in Gezer, but the Canaanites dwell among the Ephraimites to this day and have become forced laborers."*

Joshua 17:12-13 reads, *"Yet the children of Manasseh could not drive out the inhabitants of those cities; but the Canaanites would dwell in that land. 13) Yet it came to pass, when the children of Israel were waxen strong, that they put the Canaanites to tribute; but did not utterly drive them out."*

In Joshua 24:2, God has Joshua remind the people about Terah, Abraham's father, and Nachor's father: "[T]hey served other gods. Abraham served Yahweh." The "other god" that Nachor served mostly likely included Sin, the Mesopotamian moon god. This is assumed from his association with Ur in southern Mesopotamia and Haran in northern Mesopotamia (Genesis 11:31). Terah's family was polytheistic and probably worshiped one or more moon gods.

Here is where the story gets fascinating—we will see the Israelites go back and forth from worshiping only God to worshiping other gods, being punished, and returning to God—only to repeat the cycle time and time again!

The story of the Israelites during the time of the judges is a tale of recurring cycles of sin, oppression, deliverance, and peace. Each period begins with the Israelites turning away from God and embracing the worship of foreign deities, leading to their subjugation by surrounding nations. We will look at the book of Judges, which summarizes all these times.

In Judges 2:1-3, an angel of the LORD came with a message of rebuke. God reminded the Israelites that He faithfully brought them out of Egypt and gave them the land He promised their ancestors. He also made a covenant with them and expected them to keep it by not making treaties with the local people and by destroying their pagan altars. But they disobeyed. Because of their disobedience, God declared He would no longer drive out their enemies completely. Instead, the remaining nations would become a constant source of trouble and their false gods would be a trap to them.

In Judges 2:10-23 *And also all that generation were gathered unto their fathers: and there arose another generation after them, which knew not the LORD, nor yet the works which he had done for Israel. 1) And the children of Israel did evil in the sight of the LORD, and served Baalim: 12) And they forsook the LORD God of their fathers, which brought them out of the land of Egypt, and followed other gods, of the gods of the people that were round about them, and bowed themselves unto them, and provoked the LORD to anger. 13) And they forsook the LORD, and served Baal and Ashtaroth. 14) And the anger of the LORD was hot against Israel, and he delivered them into the hands of spoilers that spoiled them, and he sold them into the hands of their enemies round about, so that they could not any longer stand before their enemies. 15) Whithersoever they went out, the hand of the LORD was against them for evil, as the LORD had said, and as the LORD had sworn unto them: and they were greatly distressed. 16) Nevertheless the LORD raised up judges, which delivered them out of the hand of those that spoiled them. 17) And yet they would not hearken unto their judges, but they went a whoring after other gods, and bowed themselves unto them: they turned quickly out of the way which their fathers walked in, obeying the commandments of the LORD; but they did not so. 18) And when the LORD raised them up judges, then the LORD was with the judge, and delivered them out of the hand of their enemies all the days of the judge: for it repented the LORD because of their groanings by reason of them that oppressed them and vexed them. 19) And it came to pass, when the judge was dead, that they returned, and corrupted themselves more than their fathers, in following other gods to serve them, and to bow down unto them; they ceased not from their own doings, nor from their stubborn way. 20) And the anger of the LORD was hot against Israel; and he said, Because that this people hath transgressed my covenant which I commanded their fathers, and have not hearkened unto my voice; 21) I also will not henceforth drive out any from before them of the nations which Joshua left when he died: 22) That through them I may prove Israel, whether they will keep the way of the LORD to walk therein, as their fathers did keep it, or not. 23) Therefore the LORD left those nations, without driving them out hastily; neither delivered he them into the hand of Joshua.*

Judges 3:2-11 *Only that the generations of the children of Israel might know, to teach them war, at the least such as before knew nothing thereof; 3) Namely, five lords of the Philistines, and all the Canaanites, and the Sidonians, and the Hivites that dwelt in mount Lebanon, from mount Baalhermon unto the entering in of Hamath. 4) And they were to prove Israel by them, to know whether they would hearken unto the commandments of the LORD, which he commanded their fathers by the hand of Moses. 5) And the children of Israel dwelt among the Canaanites, Hittites, and Amorites, and Perizzites, and Hivites, and Jebusites: 6) And they took their daughters to be their wives, and gave their daughters to their sons, and served their gods. 7) And the children of Israel did evil in the sight of the LORD, and forgat the LORD their*

God, and served Baalim and the groves. 8) Therefore the anger of the LORD was hot against Israel, and he sold them into the hand of Chushanrishathaim king of Mesopotamia: and the children of Israel served Chushanrishathaim eight years. 9) And when the children of Israel cried unto the LORD, the LORD raised up a deliverer to the children of Israel, who delivered them, even Othniel the son of Kenaz, Caleb's younger brother. 10) And the Spirit of the LORD came upon him, and he judged Israel, and went out to war: and the LORD delivered Chushanrishathaim king of Mesopotamia into his hand; and his hand prevailed against Chushanrishathaim. 11) And the land had rest forty years. And Othniel the son of Kenaz died.

In the next verses (Judges 3:12-18, 30), we read: that the Israelites once again did evil in the sight of the LORD. In response, the LORD empowered Eglon, king of Moab, to rise against them. Eglon joined forces with the Ammonites and Amalekites, attacked Israel, and took control of the City of Palm Trees (Jericho). Israel served Eglon for eighteen years.

When the people cried out to the LORD, He raised up a deliverer: Ehud, the son of Gera, from the tribe of Benjamin—a man who was left-handed. Ehud was chosen to carry Israel's tribute to King Eglon. But God had a bigger plan. Ehud would go on to assassinate Eglon, leading to Israel's victory over Moab.

Verse 30: *That day, Moab was subdued under the hand of Israel, and the land enjoyed peace for eighty years.*

Judges 4:1-3 *And the children of Israel again did evil in the sight of the LORD, when Ehud was dead. 2) And the LORD sold them into the hand of Jabin king of Canaan, that reigned in Hazor; the captain of whose host was Sisera, which dwelt in Harosheth of the Gentiles. 3) And the children of Israel cried unto the LORD: for he had nine hundred chariots of iron; and twenty years he mightily oppressed the children of Israel.*

Judges 6:1 *And the children of Israel did evil in the sight of the LORD: and the LORD delivered them into the hand of Midian seven years.*

Judges 10:6-8 Once again, the Israelites did evil in the sight of the LORD. They turned to worship the gods of Baalim, Ashtaroth, and the gods of Syria, Sidon, Moab, Ammon, and the Philistines—completely abandoning the LORD and no longer serving Him. In response, the LORD's anger burned against Israel, and He allowed them to be oppressed by the Philistines and the Ammonites. That year, they crushed the Israelites and continued to oppress them for eighteen years—especially those living east of the Jordan in the land of the Amorites, which is in Gilead.

Judges 10:11-16 When the Israelites cried out for help, the LORD reminded them that He had delivered them before—from the Egyptians, the Amorites, the Ammonites, the Philistines, the Sidonians, the Amalekites, and the Maonites—every time they had cried to Him in distress. Yet they had forsaken Him again and turned to other gods. So, the LORD told them: "I will deliver you no more. Go and cry out to the gods you have chosen—let them save you in your time of trouble."

This deeply struck the Israelites. In response, they admitted their guilt and said to the LORD, "Do whatever seems good to You; just deliver us this once." Then they removed the foreign gods from among them and began serving the LORD again. And His soul was grieved for the misery of Israel.

That last line is especially moving: "His soul was grieved for the misery of Israel." What a God we serve—righteous and just, yet so tender-hearted toward His people when they truly repent.

Judges 13:1 *And the children of Israel again did that which was evil in the sight of Jehovah; and Jehovah delivered them into the hand of the Philistines forty years.*

Do you see a pattern? A generation of worshiping God but not teaching their children. Then, those children worship other gods. And God punishes them. How do you think this relates to October 7, 2023?

Samuel

In the Books of 1st and 2nd Samuel, the narrative of Israel's (and later Judah's) relationship with God revolves around their periods of faithfulness, sin, punishment, and eventual repentance, to be followed by faithfulness, sin, punishment, and eventual repentance.

The story begins with Israel under the leadership of judges, a time marked by disobedience and spiritual decay. The people often strayed from God, worshiping idols and neglecting the covenant.

The priest Eli's sons, Hophni and Phinehas, were corrupt and led Israel astray through their immoral conduct. This led to God's displeasure with Israel's leadership.

Despite warnings, the Israelites demand a king to be like other nations, showing a lack of trust in God as their true king. Samuel, the prophet, warns them of the consequences, but they insist. As a direct consequence of Israel's disobedience, the Ark of the Covenant, the symbol of God's presence, is captured by the Philistines. This symbolizes God's withdrawal of favor.

God appoints Saul as Israel's first king, but Saul quickly disobeys God's commands. His lack of faith, impatience, and incomplete obedience (like sparing King Agag and the best spoils of war in 1 Samuel 15) lead to God rejecting him as king. Saul's repeated disobedience brings turmoil. God allows Saul to continue ruling but raises up

David, a man after His own heart, to eventually succeed Saul. Saul's life is marked by jealousy, mental anguish, and ultimately his tragic death in battle against the Philistines.

David, though flawed, seeks to honor God and leads Israel to military victories and national unity. Despite Saul's opposition, God preserves David, showing His continued favor to the faithful.

In 2 Samuel, David himself falls into serious sin by committing adultery with Bathsheba and arranging the murder of her husband, Uriah. God sends the prophet Nathan to confront David. As a result, God punishes David through the death of his child with Bathsheba, ongoing family strife, and rebellion from his son Absalom. These events bring chaos to David's reign but also lead to his repentance.

After being confronted by Nathan, David humbly repents for his sins (seen in Psalm 51). Though he faces personal and national consequences, God forgives David and reaffirms His covenant with him. Despite the punishment, God restores Israel's fortunes under David's leadership. David unites the tribes and establishes Jerusalem as the political and spiritual center, securing Israel's position as a nation under God's rule.

Even after Israel and its leaders sin, God is merciful when they return to Him. Saul's downfall contrasts with David's repentance, showing the importance of seeking God's forgiveness.

The Books of Samuel highlight the tension between Israel's disobedience and God's steadfast faithfulness to His covenant. Though punishment comes, God continues to work through Israel, leading ultimately to the promise of a lasting dynasty through David.

Chronicles

Chronicles presents a different perspective on David's census compared to Samuel. In 2 Samuel 24, God's anger prompts David to conduct the census. However, in 1 Chronicles 21, Satan incites David. This change likely reflects the Chronicler's intent to preserve David's good reputation by attributing the incitement to Satan rather than an angry God.

In Chronicles, "Satan" is depicted as a celestial being acting independently of Yahweh, standing against Israel (1 Chronicles 21:1). This figure is similar to the adversary seen in Job (1:6, 2:1) and Zechariah (3:1). However, the Chronicler's Satan is distinct in actively opposing God's will.

In the Ancient Near East context, many demons and deities engaged in harmful actions towards humans. However, the closest parallel to the Satan of early Judaism and Christianity is found in Zoroastrianism, a dualistic religion from Persia.[1]

The prophet Zoroaster, who lived between the 10th and 6th centuries B.C., taught about a cosmic struggle between good, represented by Ahura Mazda, and evil, represented by Angra Mainyu

---

1. https://www.britannica.com/topic/Zoroastrianism

(Ahriman). This conflict would culminate in a final battle where good would ultimately prevail, rewarding its followers with Heaven, while those serving Angra Mainyu would be condemned to a burning hell.[2]

Zoroastrianism became the official religion of the Persian Empire during the Achaemenid dynasty (c. 559-331 B.C.) and was publicly endorsed by Darius (522-486 B.C.).

Baal Worship in Jerusalem

Of all the Canaanite deities, the Israelites were most drawn to Baal. Gideon's family, for instance, worshiped this god (Judges 6:25). When Gideon chose to worship God exclusively, he broke with his family's tradition.

In Hebrew, "Baal" translates to "lord." This title was given to the storm god, Hadad, known across Syria, Mesopotamia, and Egypt through inscriptions from the mid-3rd millennium to the last century B.C. He was typically referred to simply as "Baal."

As Baal was believed to bring rain, he was also credited with providing the annual crops dependent on rainfall. This importance led to many worship sites dedicated to Baal, each with its local variation of the god's name. There were numerous manifestations of Baal, including Baal Tamar, Baal Zephon, Baal Hermon, Baal Peor, and Baal Hadad, among many others. In addition, many families possessed their own personal Baals, represented by clay figurine idols of the deity.

Baal promised the Israelites fertility, fruitfulness, increase, gain, and prosperity. Thus, as they began cultivating the land, the temptation to invoke his powers proved increasingly compelling. Many Israelites turned away from God to follow Baal.

Baal represented everything that was opposed to God and in conflict with Him. He was the alternative deity, the substitute for God, the anti-God of Israel. Baal was the deity Israel turned to when it abandoned God. He was the one who distanced Israel from its true God, drawing the people away and causing them to forget the God of their origins.

In Ugaritic myths, Baal is depicted as a powerful, ambitious, and sometimes foolish deity who, due to his bravado, often finds himself in difficult situations. His sister, Anath, along with other gods like Kothar-and-Hasis (a skilled artisan deity), Shapsu (the sun goddess), Asherah, and El (rulers of the pantheon), frequently came to his aid.

The Israelites' devotion to Baal is evident in their reaction to Gideon's destruction of Baal's altar, where they sought to kill Gideon (Judges 6:28-30). However, his father, Joash, defended him by arguing that Baal could defend himself if he was really a god. This defense earned Gideon the nickname "Jerubbaal," meaning "let Baal contend" (Judges 6:31-32).

When the Israelites "served other Baals" (Judges 2:11), they were adopting the local culture's mythological worldview. The deities of the Syria-Palestine region formed a hierarchical structure similar to a small bureaucracy. El [Baal-Hammon] and Asherah [Baal Bub], which means "the Lady of Byblos,"[1] the top deities, were seen as the ultimate rulers of the cosmos and parents of other gods. They assigned tasks to their offspring, who made up the second level of deities.[2]

---

1. https://www.britannica.com/topic/Syrian-and-Palestinian-religion/Other-early-gods

2. Ibid.

These second-tier gods controlled natural forces, political fates, and abstract concepts like justice. They were powerful but often had conflicting interests, which explained the world's unpredictability. A third level of gods acted as craftsmen and artisans with professional expertise. They sometimes mocked the higher gods for their lack of knowledge.[3]

At the bottom of this hierarchy were messenger deities, or angels, who served as slave labor. El and Asherah could change the positions of these gods, especially if they misused their authority.

The allure of these deities sometimes proved too strong for the Israelites (Judges 2:12). Besides Asherah (Judges 3:7), they were familiar with other second-tier gods like Baal (Judges 3:7) and Anath (Judges 3:31). The idol that Hezekiah called Nehushtan (2 Kings 18:4) represented a third-level healing deity.

Samaria, Israel's capital, had a temple dedicated to Baal, as did Jerusalem, the capital of Judah (2 Chronicles 23:17). This temple in Jerusalem was possibly built by King Jehoram for his wife Athaliah, daughter of Jezebel. Athaliah brought the Baal worship from her hometown of Sidon and influenced her husband toward these practices (2 Chronicles 21:5-6).

In Jerusalem, however, Yahweh remained the primary deity. The Baal temple was for a foreign god worshiped by the royal family, similar to the temples Solomon built for his foreign wives (1 Kings 11:7-8). Worshipers of Baal likely saw him as subordinate to Yahweh, whose temple was the kingdom's central shrine.

When Athaliah seized the throne, Baal became the dominant deity. Her ruthless actions, including the murder of David's descendants (2

---

3. Ibid.

Chronicles 22:10), showed she ruled for her own protection, not as a regent for Yahweh. This possibly led to the deterioration of Yahweh's temple (2 Chronicles 24:7).

The priests of Yahweh's temple led the opposition against Athaliah. The "people of the land," likely landowners (2 Chronicles 23:13), remained loyal to Yahweh and supported the revolt to overthrow her. Restoring Yahweh's worship was crucial to ensure His protection of the land, preventing devastation like that of the northern kingdom.

Baal Worship in Samaria

The Samaritans were not total strangers to the Jewish people—they were kin. Their roots traced back to the ten northern tribes of Israel, especially Ephraim and Manasseh, sons of Joseph. But their history became one of deep fracture—politically, spiritually, and culturally.

After the kingdom of Israel split in two following Solomon's reign, the Northern Kingdom (Israel) and the Southern Kingdom (Judah) developed in very different directions. Israel, the northern territory, often fell into idolatry as its kings tried to keep their people from going to Jerusalem to worship. They set up golden calves in Bethel and Dan, and eventually opened the door to much darker practices.

During King Ahab's reign (874–853 B.C.), the Northern Kingdom still claimed to worship Yahweh, the God of Israel. But the reality on the ground was different. Baal became the dominant figure of worship—especially in the royal court—largely due to Ahab's marriage to Jezebel, a Sidonian princess (1 Kings 16:31–32). Jezebel introduced Baal worship as a formal part of Israel's national religion, and Baal's temple was built right in Samaria, the capital city (2 Kings 10:21).

Meanwhile, Yahweh's temples were located in Bethel and Dan, far from political power.

The people didn't necessarily think they had forsaken Yahweh; they simply added Baal into the mix. They believed Baal might even represent Yahweh's authority in the land. But this blending of religions—a spiritual mixture—was precisely what God had forbidden. The Law of Moses was clear: no other gods, no idols, no divided loyalties (Exodus 20:4–5). Yet the Israelites bowed before both.

This confusion and compromise may be what Jesus meant when He told the Samaritan woman,

"Ye worship ye know not what: we know what we worship: for salvation is of the Jews." (John 4:22, KJV)

They were worshiping in ignorance. Baal had no saving power, and their devotion to him brought judgment instead of blessing.

The crisis of Baalism reached its peak under Ahab. The prophet Elijah challenged Baal's prophets on Mount Carmel, and later, God raised up Jehu to bring down Baal's entire religious system. Jehu's bloody purge (2 Kings 10:18–28) wiped out the priests of Baal, destroyed his temple, and ended Baal's public worship in Israel—for a time. But the spiritual damage was done.

In 722 B.C., the Assyrian Empire conquered the Northern Kingdom. Many Israelites were exiled, and foreigners were brought in to repopulate the land. These new people intermarried with the Israelites who remained, and their descendants became the Samaritans—a mixed race with a mixed religion. They still claimed Jacob as their father and followed a version of the Pentateuch, but they rejected Jerusalem as the place of worship.

Instead, the Samaritans built their own temple on Mount Gerizim, near Shechem, and declared it the true holy site. This was partly out of religious conviction and partly out of opposition to the Jews of the Southern Kingdom, who worshiped in Jerusalem.

By Jesus' time, Jews and Samaritans were openly hostile. Jews considered Samaritans ritually unclean and spiritually compromised. Samaritans, in turn, viewed Jews as prideful and exclusive. They shared the same bloodlines and many of the same stories—but centuries of mistrust and idolatry had driven a wedge between them.

That's why Jesus' encounter with the woman at the well was so radical. When she pointed to her people's tradition of worshiping on Mount Gerizim, Jesus didn't argue about geography. Instead, He revealed a deeper truth:

"The hour cometh, when ye shall neither in this mountain, nor yet at Jerusalem, worship the Father... But the hour cometh, and now is, when the true worshippers shall worship the Father in spirit and in truth" (John 4:21, 23).

It was no longer about Samaria or Jerusalem. It was about knowing the One True God, and that knowledge would come through Jesus, the Messiah both Jews and Samaritans needed.

Other Gods

In ancient times, victorious armies often took statues and images of gods from the defeated peoples as spoils of war. For instance, two Judean kings, David and Amaziah, seized idols during their conquests—David from the Philistines (2 Samuel 5:19-21) and Amaziah from the Edomites (2 Chronicles 25:14-16).

These captured idols were often regarded as embodiments of the gods they represented. Subsequently, they were placed in the temples of the victors, symbolizing the gods' approval of the conquerors' rule. This integration of foreign deities into the conquerors' pantheon was seen as a divine endorsement of their dominance, effectively incorporating these gods into the religious framework of the empire.

For example, the cult of Marduk gained prominence as Babylonian culture spread during the Middle Babylonian-Assyrian period. Marduk was integrated into the Assyrian royal pantheon but placed after Aššur and other significant deities. Over time, Marduk absorbed the roles of other gods and became associated with Babylon's identity, symbolizing Babylonian resistance to Assyria. This rivalry influenced the elevation of Aššur in Assyria, with Aššur replacing Marduk in the Assyrian version of the Enūma eliš. Hostility between the two nations led Assyrian rulers like Sennacherib to oppose Babylon and Marduk, thereby destroying Babylon and taking Marduk's statues.

The return of these statues was seen as a sign of Babylon's revival and divine punishment of its enemies. This tension is also reflected in an Assyrian satirical composition, where Marduk undergoes a "mock trial," portraying him as a cause of conflict, much like Kingu's trial in the Enūma eliš.

Similarly, Cyrus II, the king of Persia (559-530 B.C.), gained political leverage by honoring the gods of conquered peoples. Early in his reign over Babylon, he proclaimed the return of all images taken by the Neo-Babylonian kings to their original places. Cyrus asserted that the gods had acknowledged him as the legitimate ruler of their lands.

When Amaziah adopted the Edomite gods (2 Chronicles 25:14), he was emulating a widespread practice among victorious kings. However, this act provoked the wrath of Yahweh, demonstrating that Amaziah's choice was ill-fated (2 Chronicles 25:16).

Chiun and Sikkuth (Amos 5:26) are the Hebrew words which correspond to two Accadian terms (*kayamanu* and *sakkud*), both referring to the planet Saturn. Saturn is usually depicted in Mesopotamian texts as the physical planet, used for sightings in astrological and astronomical observations. However, this would not be a reason for Israelites to carry around symbols of Saturn. This verse in Amos reads: *But ye have borne the tabernacle of your Moloch and Chiun your images, the star of your god, which ye made to yourselves.*

The Star of David has been found in archaeological sites dating from the Bronze Age (3300 – 1200 B.C.) [1] The Book of Amos was written around 786-746 B.C., [2] well after the star was adopted as

---

1. https://star-of-david.blogspot.com/2015/02/the-star-of-david-as-archaeological.html

2. https://www.britannica.com/topic/Book-of-Amos

a symbol of the Israelites. God was God and dealt with His people directly. He did not need to be represented by a star. Moloch and Chiun, on the other hand, needed something for the people "to hang onto."

Some evidence suggests that the god represented by Saturn in Mesopotamia was Ninurta (also called Nimrod). Ninurta was a warrior deity, which may explain why the Israelites carried Saturn's image. It would have made sense to carry the sign of a divine protector into battle on a standard. This was common practice with ancient armies.

Nimrod was the great-grandson of Noah and is referred to as "a mighty one in the Earth," [3] and "a mighty hunter before Jehovah." [4]

The prophet Amos uses the general terms for Saturn—Chiun and Sikkuth—rather than a specific name of the god, such as Ninurta. His choice emphasizes the foreignness of the Israelites' behavior: They were involving themselves with Assyrian religious elements. By naming a deity of Assyrian and Babylonian religion, Amos could refer obliquely to Israel's coming exile to Assyria (Amos 5:27).

Was Nimrod worshiped as a god? He was "mighty in the Earth." People obviously remembered him through several generations. So, perhaps they did.

---

3. 1 Chronicles 1:10

4. Genesis 10:9

The Book of Amos

The Judgment of False Worship—When a Nation Forgets Its God

The prophet Amos was a shepherd and fig-picker from the southern kingdom of Judah, called by God to speak to the northern kingdom of Israel during a time of prosperity and apparent peace. Outwardly, the nation was thriving. But spiritually, it was rotten at the core.

God's message through Amos was a warning to a people who had forgotten who He was, even as they continued their religious rituals.

The people of Israel were still attending the feasts, offering sacrifices, and singing praises—but God was not impressed. In fact, He rejected their worship because it came from corrupt hearts.

Amos 5:21, 23 *I hate, I despise your feast days, and I will not smell in your solemn assemblies. 23) Take thou away from me the noise of thy songs; for I will not hear the melody of thy viols.*

They thought they were honoring God, but their worship was polluted with injustice, idolatry, and arrogance. Just like their ancestors who had blended Baal worship with the name of Yahweh, they thought they could serve God and greed, God and idols, God and self—and still be safe.

The ruling class lived in luxury, oppressing the poor and perverting justice. They trusted in their strength and wealth, not in God.

"Woe to them that are at ease in Zion... that lie upon beds of ivory... but they are not grieved for the affliction of Joseph." (Amos 6:1, 4, 6, KJV)

The message was clear: complacency in times of blessing is dangerous when it's rooted in pride and self-sufficiency rather than obedience and humility.

Amos warned that God's patience was running out. Because of their unrepentant hearts, judgment would fall—not just on their enemies, but on Israel itself. The nation would fall to the sword, and the people would go into exile. Their false security and false religion had blinded them to the reality of their sin.

Amos's visions—of locusts, fire, a plumb line, and a basket of summer fruit—symbolized the end of God's long-suffering. The people had been measured and found wanting.

Yet in the middle of this strong rebuke, God still called to His people:

"Seek ye me, and ye shall live." (Amos 5:4)

Even with judgment looming, there was still a door of mercy for those who would turn back to the LORD in sincerity and truth.

The book ends with a powerful promise: after judgment, there would be restoration. God would one day raise up the tabernacle of David, and Israel would be restored under God's rule.

Amos 9:15 And I will plant them upon their land, and they shall no more be pulled up out of their land which I have given them.

This final note echoes the heart of God: true worship belongs only to the One True God, and even when His people stray, His desire is always to redeem and restore those who return to Him.

The Book of Hosea

The book of Hosea is perhaps the most intimate and emotional of all the prophetic writings. Through the life of the prophet himself, God revealed how deeply grieved and wounded He was by Israel's idolatry. The people He had redeemed and called His own were chasing after other gods, yet still speaking His name as if nothing were wrong.

It was not just a national crisis—it was a broken marriage.

Hosea lived in the northern kingdom of Israel during a time of spiritual and moral decline. God called him to deliver a profound and challenging message to the people of Israel that would unfold through the very fabric of his personal life.

God instructed Hosea to marry Gomer, a woman known for her promiscuity, to serve as a living parable of Israel's relationship with Him. Hosea obeyed, and their union produced three children, each named to reflect God's message to the nation. Their first child, a son, was named Jezreel, symbolizing God's intention to punish Israel for the bloodshed in the valley of Jezreel. Their daughter was named Lo-Ruhamah, meaning "not loved," indicating that God would no longer show love to Israel. Their third child, another son, was named

Lo-Ammi, meaning "not my people," a stark declaration that Israel had broken their covenant with God.

As Gomer strayed and became unfaithful, she mirrored the spiritual adultery of Israel, who had turned away from God to worship Baal and other idols. Despite her infidelity, Hosea's love for Gomer endured, reflecting God's steadfast love for Israel. In a powerful act of redemption, Hosea sought out Gomer, repurchased her from a life of slavery, and restored her as his wife. This act symbolized God's willingness to forgive and redeem Israel if they would only repent and return to Him.

Hosea's life and his relationship with Gomer were a poignant illustration of the accusations and judgments he proclaimed. God, speaking through Hosea, condemned Israel for their idolatry and infidelity. The nation was guilty of worshiping false gods, betraying the covenant, and committing grave social injustices. Deceit, violence, and corruption were rampant, and God's patience was wearing thin. Hosea warned of impending judgment: the nation would face exile and destruction as the consequences of their sins.

In the ancient world, the spoils of war often included statues and images of the gods from the defeated peoples. The prophet Hosea dismisses the golden calves of Samaria (Israel) by predicting that they are worthless and destined to become trophies for the Assyrians (Hosea 10:5-6).

Neo-Assyrian kings frequently documented the images of gods and gold and silver as part of the treasures seized from conquered temples. For instance, Sargon II's inscriptions record the capture of Samaria's gods among the spoils taken in 721 B.C. Although these were not the golden calves mentioned by Hosea, they were other idols used by Israel's royal house.

Captured idols held significant value, mainly for their precious metals and gems. Conquerors often dismantled these idols to demonstrate contempt for the vanquished people, repurposing the gold, silver, and gems for other uses. The wooden or stone components would be burned or shattered. In cases of extreme disdain, the entire idol would be wholly destroyed. This utter destruction explains the mourning described in Hosea 10:5.

Yet, amid these stern warnings, Hosea's message was not without hope. God's love for Israel was deep and abiding. He remembered the early days of their relationship, the tenderness of Israel's youth. God's heart was moved with compassion, and He longed for His people to return to Him. Hosea called the people to repentance, urging them to come back to God with sincere hearts. He promised that if they did, God would heal their waywardness, love them freely, and restore their fortunes.

After Shalmaneser's reign, the Neo-Assyrian Empire experienced a significant decline. By 745 B.C., its political structure was in disarray, and Urartu's kingdom seriously threatened its northern borders. A new ruler ascended to the throne at this critical juncture, initiating a resurgence of Assyrian dominance. From 744 to 681 B.C., four kings mentioned in the Bible led Assyria to its zenith of imperial power: Tiglath-Pileser III, Shalmaneser V, Sargon II, and Sennacherib.

This revival made Assyria a formidable threat to the smaller Western states. In 734 B.C., Tiglath-Pileser III launched an aggressive campaign against these states, culminating in the conquest of Damascus in 732 B.C. and compelling most other states to pay tribute to Assyria.

A decade later, the Assyrians besieged Samaria, Israel's capital, ultimately leading to its downfall. Shalmaneser V led a three-year siege that resulted in Samaria's fall in 722 B.C. Sargon II succeeded Shalmaneser in the same year and is likely the king who exiled the Israelites, fulfilling Hosea's prophecy:

Hosea 11:5 *He shall not return into the land of Egypt, but the Assyrian shall be his king, because they refused to return.*

Assyria's resurgence as a major power was swift and impactful. Sennacherib (704-681 B.C.) captured most of Judah's significant towns in the 701 B.C. campaign and destroyed Babylon in 689 B.C.

Do you see the pattern continuing?

Manasseh's reign (697-642 B.C.) was the longest in the history of the Judean kingdom. In the first 11 or 12 years, he ruled as a minor, serving as a co-regent with his father, Hezekiah. Manasseh faced criticism for worshiping the stars—the "host of Heaven" (2 Kings 21:3). Some scholars believe Assyria influenced his religious practices, as vassal states were required to pay tribute and swear loyalty oaths, demonstrating their allegiance to Assyrian rule. However, no evidence exists that Assyria imposed its religion on these states. It is possible that Manasseh voluntarily incorporated Assyrian cultic practices in the temple to show his loyalty to Assyria.

The writer of Chronicles notes that Manasseh was taken prisoner by the Assyrians and sent to Babylon (2 Chronicles 33:11). Although Babylon did not gain significant power until after 625 B.C., several years after Manasseh's reign, it is plausible that he could have been sent there. After the death of Esarhaddon, the Assyrians had co-rulers in Nineveh and Babylon for 16 years (668-652 B.C.), making it possible for Manasseh to have been detained in Babylon during that period.

When Manasseh died, he was replaced by his son, Amon (642-640 B.C.). Amon was assassinated in the royal palace. After executing those who had conspired against Amon, the people of the land made his son, Josiah, king. Josiah was eight years old when he became king and reigned 31 years in Jerusalem (1 Kings 22:1). The big difference was that Josiah returned to the Lord God and did what was right in the sight of the Lord (v. 2).

The Book of Hosea speaks just as loudly to modern Israel and the world today. We see nations—including God's own people—chasing after other gods: materialism, self-worship, false religions, sensuality, and spiritual compromise. The world says, "It's all love," but Hosea shows us that God calls compromise adultery—and He grieves over it.

Just as Hosea bought back his unfaithful wife, Jesus paid the price to redeem His bride, the Church. He is still calling us—not to blend Him with other beliefs—but to come back fully. Back to truth. Back to covenant. Back to Him.

The Book of Zephaniah

In the days of King Josiah of Judah, a prophet named Zephaniah emerged with a message from the Lord. Zephaniah, a descendant of King Hezekiah, carried a heavy burden: he was to announce the coming judgment of God upon Judah and the surrounding nations.

Zephaniah's prophecy began with a dire warning of the approaching "Day of the Lord." Christians think the "Day of the Lord" will be wonderful. However, the Bible indicates it will be a day of immense darkness and destruction, when God's wrath will sweep through the land, wiping out all idolatry and corruption that had taken root.

The people had turned their backs on God, worshiping false idols and living in wickedness. Zephaniah described the coming devastation in vivid, terrifying terms, urging the people to recognize the seriousness of their sin.

The prophet's message did not stop with Judah. Zephaniah's vision extended to the nations around Judah—Philistia, Moab, Ammon, Cush, and even the mighty Assyria. In their pride and violence, each of these nations had provoked God's anger. They, too, would face His judgment. Their cities would be laid waste, their peoples brought low, and their lands desolate.

Yet, amid these grim warnings, Zephaniah's message also carried a glimmer of hope. He turned his attention back to Jerusalem, condemning its leaders, prophets, and priests for their relentless corruption and disobedience. Despite the repeated warnings and opportunities to repent, they continued in their sinful ways, ignoring God's call to righteousness.

But God, in His mercy, would not utterly destroy His people. Zephaniah spoke of a time beyond the judgment, a time when God would purify the lips of the people so they could call on His name and serve Him faithfully. A remnant of humble and righteous people would be preserved. These survivors, refined by the trials of judgment, would live in a restored Jerusalem, a city of honor and joy.

In a beautiful, uplifting vision, Zephaniah described a future where God Himself would dwell among His people. He would remove their fear and shame and rejoice over them with singing. This divine love and forgiveness would bring about the ultimate redemption of God's people, turning their sorrow into joy and their despair into hope.

Thus, Zephaniah's message, while heavy with warnings of impending doom, also shone with the promise of restoration and God's enduring love for those who turn to Him with sincere hearts. The prophet's words served as both a sobering reminder of the consequences of sin and a comforting assurance of God's unwavering commitment to redeem and restore His people.

The prophet Zephaniah foretells judgment upon the people of Judah due to their apostasy and pursuit of other deities, incurring Yahweh's wrath. Baal, also known as the storm god Hadad, was a prominent Canaanite deity reintroduced in Jerusalem during Manasseh's reign (2 Kings 21:3). Zephaniah 1:4 warns of the eradication of Baal's presence, reminiscent of actions in Egypt post-Amarna period (c. 1336 B.C.) where the name of Aten was chiseled out from monuments and manuscripts. God, through Zephaniah, threatens even more severe measures—not just the removal of Baal's name but the destruction of his worshipers.

Additionally, some worshiped the host of Heaven in their homes, indicating a belief in a pantheon of gods. Zephaniah 1:5 describes them worshiping "on the housetops," likely while observing the stars, suggesting family worship services for various deities in personal homes rather than in cultic centers.

Many in Judah attempted to worship multiple gods alongside Yahweh. Zephaniah mentions Milcom (or Molech) in Zephaniah 1:5, highlighting the people's deviation from the exclusive worship of Yahweh. Who was Molech? His name means *the abomination*.[1] He required human sacrifice, mainly by having children "pass through the fire."[2] When child sacrifice became commonplace, even though it horrified the ancient world, the practice of sacrificing a child to any deity became known as a "Molech sacrifice." Jeremiah denounced both the practice of child sacrifice and the city of Jerusalem for permitting it (Jeremiah 7:30-32, 19:13).

The Tophet was a cult site in the Valley of Hinnom, near Jerusalem, where human sacrifices were conducted. Two Judahite kings, Ahaz (2 Chronicles 28:1-3) and Manasseh (2 Chronicles 33:1, 6), are recorded as having sacrificed children there. It is unclear whether Jeremiah witnessed the worship of Molech or the integration of Molech's child

---

1. 33 Cahn, Jonathan, The Return of the Gods, Frontline, an imprint of Chrisma Media, 2022, 95

2. Leviticus 18;21; Deuteronomy 18:10; 2 Kings 26:3; 2 Kings 17:17, 21:6, 23:10; 2 Chronicles 33:6; Jeremiah 32:35; Ezekiel 26:21, 20:26, 20:21, 23:37

sacrifice into the worship of Yahweh. However, the prophet regarded it as a grave abomination (Jeremiah 32:35).

While oaths in other nations involved swearing by multiple deities to ensure seriousness, Zephaniah condemns any oath appealing to other gods as false, affirming that Yahweh alone should be the sole deity acknowledged by Judah.

During Josiah's reign, the priests and prophets were eager for a revival of worship, culminating in the grand celebration of the Passover in 622 B.C., marking the pinnacle of Josiah's religious reforms (2 Kings 23:21-23).

Josiah also inspired hope among Judahites with secular ambitions, particularly those aspiring to reunite Israel. He began expanding Judah's territory into areas that had been part of the northern kingdom of Israel before its capture by Assyria. This expansion was facilitated by the significant decline of the Assyrian Empire, which left a power vacuum in the former northern kingdom. One notable action by Josiah was the destruction of the idolatrous Israelite shrine at Bethel, from which the prophet Amos had been expelled over a century earlier (Amos 7:10-17).

The Hebrew term translated as "high place" refers to a sanctuary. Solomon had built temples to foreign gods near Jerusalem, officially incorporating these deities into the religion of Israel. In the ancient Near East, any religious site constructed by the reigning ruler was considered state sanctioned. Solomon constructed such sanctuaries extensively, as he built shrines for all his foreign wives (1 Kings 11:5-8).

Three deities—Ashtoreth, Chemosh, and Milcom—had high places constructed by Solomon (2 Kings 23:13). Ashtoreth (or Astarte) was the patron goddess of Sidon, a powerful Phoenician city-state. Chemosh was the patron god of Moab, and an inscription from around 850 B.C. recounts Chemosh and the Moabite king Mesha's victory over Israel. Milcom (or Molech), the god of Ammon, required human sacrifice. Solomon, a prominent figure, allowed these deities into Israel, but Josiah famously eradicated them.

Chemosh was the national deity of the Moabites, an ancient people who lived in the region now known as Jordan. He is frequently mentioned in the Hebrew Bible and is depicted as a god to whom the Moabites offered sacrifices, including human sacrifices in some instances. Chemosh is particularly noted for being worshiped by King Solomon's foreign wives, which led Solomon to construct high places for himself and other foreign deities, much to the disapproval of the Biblical writers.

An important historical reference to Chemosh comes from the Mesha Stele (or Moabite Stone), an inscribed stone set up around 850 B.C. by King Mesha of Moab. The stele celebrates Chemosh's supposed victory over Israel and details Mesha's construction of cities and sanctuaries in Chemosh's honor. This artifact provides insight into the religious practices and beliefs of the Moabites and highlights Chemosh's central role in their society.

Judgment Begins at the House of God Zephaniah 1:4–6 *I will also stretch out mine hand upon Judah, and upon all the inhabitants of Jerusalem; and I will cut off the remnant of Baal from this place, and the name of the Chemarims with the priests; 5) And them that worship the host of heaven upon the housetops; and them that worship and that swear by the LORD, and that swear by Malcham; 6) And them that are turned back from the LORD; and those that have not sought the LORD, nor enquired for him.*

This echoes 1 Peter 4:17, which says judgment begins at the house of God. Zephaniah's warning wasn't just for the pagan nations—it was for God's people who had grown complacent, mixed in idolatry, and stopped seeking Him. That's us, right now. In many modern churches, truth is watered down, and the fear of the Lord is absent. Zephaniah's warning calls believers to wake up and return wholeheartedly to God.

"The great day of the Lord is near... a day of wrath, a day of trouble and distress..." (Zephaniah 1:14-15)

The phrase "Day of the Lord" appears throughout prophetic books and is closely tied to end-time judgment. Zephaniah's description sounds eerily like what Jesus and the Book of Revelation describe—economic collapse, environmental distress, fear gripping nations. We're seeing birth pangs now: natural disasters, moral decline, wars, lawlessness. This isn't just history—it's prophecy repeating itself in waves.

The Book of Ezekiel

The prophet Ezekiel highlighted a specific type of religious practice to proclaim judgment on the Judeans. In various ancient Near Eastern religions of Mesopotamia and Syria-Palestine, priestesses participated in ritual prostitution as part of their religious duties. Although the exact reasons and methods of these acts are unclear, Ezekiel accused the Judeans of engaging in a similar form of prostitution by devoting themselves to gods other than Yahweh. He stated they had "played the harlot" with these other deities' representatives (Ezekiel 16:15-17). Ezekiel rebuked the Judeans for pursuing gods from Canaan, Egypt, and Assyria, forsaking Yahweh, who had provided for them. The Canaanite gods, especially Asherah and Baal, were worshiped throughout the monarchies of Israel and Judah. The food given by Yahweh was used to worship Baal, the storm god believed to bring fertility and grain (Ezekiel 16:19).

Egyptian deities had been worshiped in Palestine since at least the era of Egyptian dominance in the 2nd millennium B.C. Images of Hathor and Bes were present in the region through Judah's monarchy. Some Judeans might have turned to Egyptian gods in Judah's final days, hoping these deities of their political ally would aid them against

Nebuchadnezzar II (Ezekiel 16:26). Throughout Judah's history, the nation sought alliances with stronger powers—Assyria (Ezekiel 16:28) and Babylonia [Chaldea] (Ezekiel 16:29)—both politically and militarily, due to a lack of faith in Yahweh as their protector. These alliances often required acknowledging the gods of these nations. Some Judeans worshiped these foreign gods, believing that they had triumphed over Yahweh and now ruled the universe. As a result, Judah had indeed become "a brazen harlot" (Ezekiel 16:30).

The book of Ezekiel contains several instances of the Jews turning away from God, facing punishment, and then returning to God, only to repeat the cycle. Ezekiel, a prophet during the Babylonian exile, often addressed the Israelites' recurring unfaithfulness and the consequent judgments from God.

Throughout the book, Ezekiel condemns the Israelites for their idolatry. In Ezekiel 8, the prophet is shown visions of the abominations being committed in the temple, which included idol worship. This idolatry leads to God's departure from the temple and the city, signifying His withdrawal of protection and blessing.

As a result of their persistent disobedience and idolatry, God allowed the Babylonians to conquer Jerusalem and take the Jews into exile. Ezekiel 5 and 6 describe the severe judgments that would fall upon Jerusalem, including famine, pestilence, and sword, as punishment for their sins.

Despite the harsh judgments, God also promises restoration. Ezekiel 36 speaks of God's intention to gather the Israelites from among the nations, cleanse them from their impurities, and give them a new heart and spirit. This indicates a return to God and a renewal of their relationship.

In Ezekiel 37, the vision of the valley of dry bones symbolizes Israel's spiritual revival. God brings the dry bones to life, representing the nation's restoration. This vision emphasizes God's power to revive and restore His people even after severe punishment.

The cycle of rebellion and restoration is a recurring theme. Ezekiel 20 recounts Israel's history of rebellion from the time of their exodus from Egypt to their current exile. Each time, God punishes them but also shows mercy and offers a path to repentance and restoration.

These patterns highlight the Israelites' ongoing struggle to remain faithful to God and the consequences of their disobedience. However, they also emphasize God's enduring mercy and willingness to restore His people when they turn back to Him.

The Book of Isaiah

Isaiah, a major prophet in the Old Testament, prophesied during the reigns of Kings Uzziah, Jotham, Ahaz, and Hezekiah of Judah (Isaiah 1:1). His messages addressed the people's sins, warned of impending judgment, and offered hope of restoration.

In the Book of Isaiah, the story of Israel (the northern kingdom) and Judah (the southern kingdom) unfolds like a powerful drama of rebellion, warning, judgment, and hope. The people, chosen by God and led out of slavery in Egypt, were meant to be a shining example of faithfulness to Him. Yet, over time, they turned their hearts away from God, chasing after other gods, adopting unjust practices, and forsaking the covenant that had made them His people.

In the opening chapters, the prophet Isaiah confronts Judah with their sins. They have become a rebellious nation and full of hypocrisy. They still perform religious rituals, but their hearts are far from God. The people have grown corrupt, the leaders have turned to injustice, and the rich have oppressed the poor. Their cities are filled with violence, and they rely on alliances with foreign powers like Egypt and Assyria for protection instead of trusting in God. Isaiah calls them to repentance, pleading with them to "wash and make yourselves clean" (Isaiah 1:16), but they refuse to listen.

As time passes, both Israel and Judah face the consequences of their rebellion. The northern kingdom, Israel, falls to the Assyrian Empire as God allows their enemies to conquer them. Judah, too, is warned of impending judgment if they do not return to God. Isaiah speaks of a coming disaster, where Jerusalem will be laid low, and the people will face exile because of their disobedience. Yet, even amid this dire warning, God's heart of compassion shines through.

Isaiah also speaks of hope, offering a vision of when the people will return to God. He speaks of a "remnant"—a small group who will survive the coming judgment and return to God with sincere hearts. These faithful few will help rebuild what was lost. In this future, Isaiah envisions a king from the line of David who will reign in righteousness, bringing peace and justice to Israel and all nations. This king, whom Isaiah calls "Immanuel" (meaning "God with us"), will be a light to the world and a sign of God's enduring love for His people.

The exile comes, as Isaiah predicted. Judah is taken into captivity in Babylon, and their beloved city of Jerusalem destroyed. Nevertheless, even in exile, God does not abandon them. Through Isaiah, He promises that this exile will not be the end. God's love for His people is unshakable, and He promises to bring them back home. Isaiah speaks of the day when they will be comforted and restored. God declares, "Comfort, comfort my people" (Isaiah 40:1), and Isaiah's voice becomes a beacon of hope. He foretells that when the exiles return, the desert will bloom, and their sins will be forgiven.

The people's hearts are humbled in exile, and eventually, as Isaiah prophesied, they are allowed to return to their land. They rebuild Jerusalem, restore the temple, and seek to follow God again. However, Isaiah's vision extends far beyond this physical return. He points to the ultimate redemption, a time when God's servant will come, bearing the people's sins and bringing salvation not just for Israel and Judah but for the entire world. Though rejected and suffering, this servant will bring healing and forgiveness through his sacrifice, fulfilling God's plan to restore His people fully to Himself..

Thus, the story of Israel and Judah in Isaiah is one of heartbreak and hope. They turned away from God and suffered the consequences, but God's promise of redemption and restoration remains constant. Even in their darkest moments, God's love shines through, and the book closes with the hope of a future where God will restore not just His people but all creation in a new heaven and new Earth where righteousness reigns forever.

Isaiah 24:1 *Behold, the LORD maketh the Earth empty, and maketh it waste, and turneth it upside down, and scattereth abroad the inhabitants thereof. 2) And it shall be, as with the people, so with the priest; as with the servant, so with his master; as with the maid, so with her mistress; as with the buyer, so with the seller; as with the lender, so with the borrower; as with the taker of usury, so with the giver of usury to him. 3) The land shall be utterly emptied, and utterly spoiled: for the LORD hath spoken this word. 4) The Earth mourneth and fadeth away, the world languisheth and fadeth away, the haughty people of the Earth do languish. 5) The Earth also is defiled under the inhabitants thereof; because they have transgressed the laws, changed the ordinance, broken the everlasting covenant. 6) Therefore hath the curse devoured the earth, and they that dwell therein are desolate:* therefore the inhabitants of the Earth are burned, and few men left.

Isaiah is so rich with prophetic insight that it's almost like reading today's headlines with spiritual commentary!

The Book of Malachi

The book of Malachi tells a compelling story set during a spiritual and moral decline among the Jewish people after their return from the Babylonian exile. The narrative unfolds with the voice of the prophet Malachi, whose name means "my messenger," delivering God's messages to His wayward people.

When the people of Israel felt abandoned and questioned God's love, Malachi began his prophetic mission by affirming God's unwavering love for them. He contrasted this love with the judgment upon Edom, their persistent enemy, to remind the Israelites of God's special relationship with them.

However, Malachi's affirmations quickly turned into rebukes. He targeted the priests, the very leaders who were supposed to guide the people in worship. These priests had shown contempt for God by offering blemished and unacceptable sacrifices. Instead of leading with integrity, they had failed their sacred duty. God, through Malachi, warned that their blessings would be cursed and that they would be humiliated and despised unless they honored their covenant with Him.

The prophet then turned his attention to the broader community, condemning their unfaithfulness in marriage and their disregard for the covenant. The men of Israel had married foreign women who worshiped other gods, leading to a dilution of their faith and culture. They had also been divorcing their wives, breaking the sacred bond of marriage. This betrayal caused societal disintegration and invoked God's displeasure. Malachi called the people to return to faithfulness, both to their spouses and to their God.

The narrative deepened as Malachi addressed the people's growing skepticism about God's justice. They complained that evildoers seemed to prosper while the righteous suffered. In response, Malachi promised that a messenger would come to prepare the way for the Lord, who would then come to His temple to purify and judge. This divine intervention would cleanse the priests and the people, distinguishing between the righteous and the wicked.

One of the most poignant moments in Malachi's message was his accusation that the people were robbing God by withholding their tithes and offerings. This disobedience had led to a curse on their land, resulting in economic hardship and poor harvests. Yet, even in His reprimand, God extended a promise of restoration. If the people would bring their full tithes into the storehouse, He would open the windows of heaven, pouring out blessings so abundant that there would not be room enough to store them.

As Malachi's story approached its climax, he addressed the cynical belief that serving God was futile. God reassured the faithful that their deeds were remembered and recorded in a scroll of remembrance. A day of reckoning was coming when the wicked would be punished, and the righteous would shine like the sun.

The narrative concluded with a call to remember the law of Moses and a prophetic promise. God declared that He would send the prophet Elijah before the great and dreadful day of the Lord. (Notice, once again, "The Day of the Lord" is a "great and dreadful day.") This messenger would work to turn the hearts of parents to their children and the hearts of children to their parents, preventing the land from being struck with a curse.

To summarize, the book of Malachi is a powerful narrative of confrontation, warning, and hope. It tells the story of a people who had strayed from their God, faced the consequences, and were called back to faithfulness. Through Malachi, God reminded His people of His enduring love and offered them a path to restoration and blessing, provided they returned to Him with sincere hearts and obedience. The book ends with a forward-looking promise of a future messenger who would herald a new era of reconciliation and renewal, setting the stage for the coming of the Messiah.

Surrounded by their enemies

Historically speaking, there have been several times when God's people were surrounded by their enemies, for God to intervene and "save the day!"

Starting with Exodus 14:10-31, the Israelites were trapped between Pharaoh's army and the Red Sea. The Israelites cried out to the Lord. He instructed Moses to stretch out his hand over the sea. The waters were divided, and the Israelites went through the sea on dry ground. As the Egyptians came after them, the walls collapsed, drowning the Egyptian army.

In 2 Chronicles 20:1-30, King Jehoshaphat and Judah were threatened by a vast army of Moabites, Ammonites, and Meunims (the people of Mount Seir). But God told the king, "Do not be afraid or discouraged because of this vast army. For the battle is not yours, but God's" (2 Chronicles 20:15). As the people began to sing and praise God, the Lord set ambushes against the men of Ammon and Moab and Mount Seir, and they were defeated (2 Chronicles 20:22).

Gideon's victory over the Midianites is recorded in Judges 7:1-25. God told Gideon, "You have too many men. I cannot deliver Midian into your hands, or Israel would boast against me that their own strength saved them (Judges 7:2). God told Gideon to divide the men into three companies. He placed trumpets and empty jars in the hands of all of them, with torches inside (Judges 7:16). When the three hundred trumpets sounded, the Lord caused the men throughout the enemy's camp to turn on each other with their swords, and the army fled. (Judges 7:22).

Then, there was the story of David and Goliath in 1 Samuel 17:1-51 and Hezekiah's deliverance from Sennacherib in 2 Kings 19:32-36.

All these passages illustrate times when enemies surrounded the Israelites, they faced potential destruction, and they experienced miraculous deliverance through God's intervention.

The End Times

The prophetic books of the Old Testament that tell about the end-times when Israel will be surrounded by her enemies and being attacked on all sides and then God steps in to intervene, include the Book of Zechariah (12:1-9, 14:1-5), Ezekiel (chapters 38 and 39), Joel (3:1-2, 9-16), Isaiah (66:15-16), and Micah (4:11-13). These passages collectively portray a scenario where Israel, particularly Jerusalem, faces a formidable threat from surrounding nations, only to be delivered by divine intervention. They highlight the themes of judgment, deliverance, and the ultimate victory of God's people in the end-times.

To clarify what has happened with Israel, I offer the following:

On October 7, 2023, thousands of rockets bombarded Israel from various directions while Hamas fighters invaded by land, sea, and air. Hundreds of people were killed and kidnapped, with methods resembling those of ISIS: targeting young women and children, launching indiscriminate rocket attacks on civilian areas, and infiltrating cities and settlements near the Gaza border.

The attackers went door to door, searching for the young and the elderly, taking hostages. Among those captured were elderly women, young children, and Holocaust survivors. The latest death toll stands at 62,614 Palestinians and 1,139 people killed in Israel since October

7, 2023 [1], a number that is expected to rise. This unprecedented attack prompted Israeli Prime Minister Benjamin Netanyahu to declare, "We are at war."

Hamas, a terrorist organization funded by Iran, orchestrated this attack. Iran has long aimed to destroy Israel and is reportedly developing nuclear weapons, frequently threatening to annihilate Israel. An Iranian leader once stated, "The regime that is occupying Jerusalem must be wiped off the map." [2]

Remarkably, Jerusalem remains the focal point of end-times prophecies. In Zechariah 12:3-4, the Bible foretells that Jerusalem will be a stumbling block for nations, a prophecy seemingly fulfilled today.

Recently, the U.S. administration, under President Biden, provided Iran with six billion dollars—a controversial move considering Iran's support for global terrorism.

Bible prophecy scholars should note that the re-establishment of Israel in 1948 marked a significant prophetic milestone. After the Holocaust, the unlikely return of the Jewish people to their homeland led to the recognition of Israel as a nation, with the U.S. being the first to acknowledge it.

Post-regathering, the Bible predicts attacks on Israel. Ezekiel 37 and 38 describe a northern force, identified as Gog and Magog (often thought to be Russia and China, but potentially modern-day Europe) attacking Israel.

---

1. https://www.aljazeera.com/news/longform/2023/10/9/israel-hamas-war-in-maps-and-charts-live-tracker

2. Quoted in Iran: The Coming Crisis by Mark Hitchcock (Multnomah, 2010)

If Israel were to strike Iran in retaliation, it could trigger a conflict resembling the prophecy in Ezekiel 38, where Magog, along with Persia, is drawn into a confrontation with Israel. The question arises, "Who are the current countries that were part of the old Persian Empire?" Persia stretched from the Northeast area of Egypt all the way to the border of India. Those countries are now:

Iran – The heartland of the Persian Empire.

Iraq – Included the ancient region of Mesopotamia.

Turkey – Especially the eastern and central parts, including Anatolia.

Syria – Part of the western territories of the empire.

Lebanon – Included in the empire's Mediterranean coastal regions.

Israel and Palestine – Part of the empire's holdings along the eastern Mediterranean.

Jordan – Covered as part of the broader Levant region.

Egypt – Controlled by Persia during specific periods.

Afghanistan – Part of the eastern territories.

Pakistan – Especially the western parts, including the region of Balochistan.

Uzbekistan – Included as part of the empire's northern territories.

Turkmenistan – Also part of the empire's northeastern regions.

Tajikistan – Included in the eastern frontiers of the empire.

Kuwait – Part of the Persian Gulf region.

Bahrain – The empire extended into the Persian Gulf islands.

Oman – The empire's eastern edge included parts of the Arabian Peninsula.

United Arab Emirates – Also part of the empire's influence along the Persian Gulf.

Armenia – Part of the northern territories of the Persian Empire.

Azerbaijan – Covered by the empire, including the areas of the Caucasus.

Georgia – Included in the empire's control of the Caucasus region.

Kazakhstan – The western parts of the empire were within its reach at its height.

While this scenario is speculative, the alignment of current events with Biblical prophecy is noteworthy.

Considering these events, Christians are encouraged to heed Jesus' words: "Now when these things begin to happen, look up and lift up your heads, because your redemption draws near" (Luke 21:28 NKJV). Additionally, they should pray for the peace of Jerusalem (Psalm 122:6), for an end to terrorism, and for the protection of Israel during this critical time.

As I listened to the news this morning, I heard that the Jewish people were returning to the synagogues in droves. This is a repeat of history.

Do you remember after 9/11? The Christian churches were filled to capacity. It lasted for about three weeks, and then people drifted away again. There had been no more attacks, and they felt secure in their homes, cities, states, and country.

9/11 may have been only a warning. Things have been downhill since then. Will there be more attacks in our future?

But, what about the Book of Revelation?

I'm glad you asked!

The Book of Revelation

Revelation Chapter 13 sets the stage for the ultimate confrontation between good and evil, leading up to the final triumph of God's kingdom, as described in the subsequent chapters of Revelation. In the vision that John saw and recorded in Revelation Chapter 13, a dramatic and terrifying scene unfolded, rich with symbolism and profound meaning. The following gives excerpts from Revelation: What John Knew:

Revelation 19:19 *And I saw the beast, and the kings of the Earth, and their armies, gathered together to make war against him that sat on the horse, and against his army.*

The kings of the Earth have united with Satan and the false religion. They fight against God and Christ.

In Revelation 17:14, we see that this war is coming and that The Lamb will win.

Revelation 19:20 *And the beast was taken, and with him the false prophet that wrought miracles before him, with which he deceived them that had received the mark of the beast, and them that worshiped his image. These both were cast alive into a lake of fire burning with brimstone.*

This was not the Hebrew Sheol, which is the grave. This was a lake of fire. This is the image we Christians think of when we think of hell.

Revelation 19:21 *And the remnant were slain with the sword of him that sat upon the horse, which sword proceeded out of his mouth: and all the fowls were filled with their flesh.*

The remnant—those left on Earth—are slain by the Word of God, and the birds have their supper.

These verses from Revelation picture the prophecies from the Old Testament, which speak of Israel being surrounded by her enemies, attacked on every side, and almost destroyed, with God intervening at the last moment to win.

The Old Testament contains several books, chapters, and verses that are often interpreted as referring to attacks on Israel in the end-times. These prophecies are found in both the major and minor prophetic books. Here are some critical references:

Isaiah chapters 24-27 are sometimes called "The Isaiah Apocalypse." These chapters describe a time of global judgment and deliverance for Israel.

Isaiah, Chapter 34, speaks of the judgment against the nations, particularly Edom. The ancient kingdom of Edom was in a region that is now part of modern-day Jordan. Specifically, Edom was situated to the south of the Dead Sea, extending into the mountainous areas of southern Jordan and possibly parts of the Negev desert in modern-day Israel. The city of Petra, famous today, was later inhabited by the Nabataeans in what was once Edomite territory.

Jeremiah, chapters 30-31, are known as the "Book of Consolation." These chapters describe a future restoration for Israel after a period of great distress.

Ezekiel chapters 38-39 detail the prophecy against Gog and Magog, describing a massive invasion of Israel and God's intervention. At one time, Russia and Iran had a pact whereby if Iran were attacked, Russia would come to her aid. However, that pact expired in 2021, having run its agreed upon 20-year course. But, be advised, on January 21, 2025, Russia and Iran signed a new pact that does not include any military alliance or require any obligations of either side.

Many Bible scholars and prophecy watchers have long connected Ezekiel 38–39 with a future military alliance between Russia ("Gog of the land of Magog") and Persia (modern-day Iran). The prophecy describes a coalition from the far north attacking Israel, with devastating consequences—but ultimately, God intervenes and defends His people.

In 2001, when Russia and Iran strengthened ties, it seemed this coalition might be forming in real time. When I wrote my first book, *Revelation: What John Knew*, this pact was fully in place and I believed (and still believe) it could have been I place for fulfillment of the Ezekiel prophecy.

So, when Russia and Iran signed another "strategic" treaty in 2025, some asked: Is this the moment Ezekiel foresaw?

Not quite.

While the new agreement formalizes the relationship between Moscow and Tehran, it stops short of creating a military alliance. Unlike Russia's treaty with North Korea, the 2025 Russia–Iran pact:

Contains no mutual defense clause

Does not commit either nation to military aid if the other is attacked

Largely reaffirms existing economic and political ties

Though military cooperation continues in areas like intelligence and joint exercises, the absence of any pledge to attack or defend signals this is not yet the fulfillment of Ezekiel's war.

Still, the groundwork is being laid. The two nations are increasingly aligned, not by friendship, but by shared isolation from the West. Should deeper military pacts or shared aggression toward Israel emerge, this treaty may come to be seen not as the war itself—but as the setup before the storm.

Prophetic Watchpoint:

Ezekiel's war is not triggered by diplomacy—it's triggered by opportunity, greed, and deception.

This treaty may simply be the rehearsal, not the opening act.

Daniel chapter 7 describes the vision of four beasts representing kingdoms and the ultimate victory of God's kingdom.

Daniel 9:24-27 *Seventy weeks are determined upon thy people and upon thy holy city, to finish the transgression, and to make an end of sins, and to make reconciliation for iniquity, and to bring in everlasting righteousness, and to seal up the vision and prophecy, and to anoint the most Holy. 25) Know therefore and understand, that from the going forth of the commandment to restore and to build Jerusalem unto the Messiah the Prince shall be seven weeks, and threescore and two weeks: the street shall be built again, and the wall, even in troublous times. 26) And after threescore and two weeks shall Messiah be cut off, but not for himself: and the people of the prince that shall come shall destroy the city and the sanctuary; and the end thereof shall be with a flood, and unto the end of the war desolations are determined. 27) And he shall confirm the covenant with many for one week: and in the midst of the week he shall cause the sacrifice and the oblation to cease, and for the overspreading of abominations he shall make it desolate, even until the consummation, and that determined shall be poured upon the desolate.*

Daniel, chapters 11-12, cover conflicts involving Israel and culminate in a description of the end-times.

Joel, chapters 2-3, describes a locust plague as a metaphor for an invading army and speaks of the "Day of the Lord" and the judgment of the nations.

Zechariah, chapters 12-14, describe a future siege of Jerusalem and Israel's eventual victory through divine intervention.

Jeremiah 30:7 refers to a time of great trouble for Jacob (Israel), often interpreted as the end-times: *Alas! for that day is great, so that none is like it: it is even the time of Jacob's trouble; but he shall be saved out of it.*

Ezekiel 38:8-12: Details the invasion of Israel by Gog and Magog:

Ezekiel 38:8-12 *After many days thou shalt be visited: in the latter years thou shalt come into the land that is brought back from the sword, and is gathered out of many people, against the mountains of Israel, which have been always waste: but it is brought forth out of the nations, and they shall dwell safely all of them. 9) Thou shalt ascend and come like a storm, thou shalt be like a cloud to cover the land, thou, and all thy bands, and many people with thee. 10) Thus saith the Lord GOD; It shall also come to pass, that at the same time shall things come into thy mind, and thou shalt think an evil thought: 11) And thou shalt say, I will go up to the land of unwalled villages; I will go to them that are at rest, that dwell safely, all of them dwelling without walls, and having neither bars nor gates, 12) To take a spoil, and to take a prey; to turn thine hand upon the desolate places that are now inhabited, and upon the people that are gathered out of the nations, which have gotten cattle and goods, that dwell in the midst of the land.*

Daniel 9:26-27: Speaks of the end-times desolation:

Daniel 9:26-27 *And after threescore and two weeks shall Messiah be cut off, but not for himself: and the people of the prince that shall come shall destroy the city and the sanctuary; and the end thereof shall be with a flood, and unto the end of the war desolations are determined. 27)*

And he shall confirm the covenant with many for one week: and in the midst of the week he shall cause the sacrifice and the oblation to cease, and for the overspreading of abominations he shall make it desolate, even until the consummation, and that determined shall be poured upon the desolate.

In Joel 2:1-11, Joel opens with an urgent warning: "Blow the trumpet in Zion!" A day of judgment—the Day of the Lord—is fast approaching, and it will be like no other. It is a day of darkness and gloom, clouds and thick darkness. A vast and powerful army is coming, unlike any ever seen before—or ever will be again.

This invading force moves with terrifying precision. They devour everything in their path like a consuming fire. What was once like the Garden of Eden before them becomes a desolate wilderness after they pass. Nothing escapes.

They charge like mighty warriors. They scale walls like soldiers. They don't break ranks or jostle one another; each stays in his path, unshaken and unstoppable. They rush into the city, run on the walls, climb into houses, and enter like thieves through windows.

As they advance, the earth quakes, the heavens tremble, the sun and moon darken, and the stars no longer shine.

This isn't just an earthly army—it's part of God's divine judgment. The Lord Himself leads this army, and His voice goes before them. The day is great and very terrible, and Joel asks, "Who can abide it?"

Zechariah 12:3 speaks of all nations gathering against Jerusalem.

Zechariah 14:2-3: Describes the siege of Jerusalem and the Lord's intervention.

Zechariah 14:8-21 describes what happens when God wins the battle:

After the Lord returns and defeats the enemies of Jerusalem, a new era begins—a time of restoration, holiness, and divine rule.

Living waters will flow out of Jerusalem—half toward the eastern sea and half toward the western sea—symbolizing abundant life, cleansing, and healing, continuing summer and winter, showing it's a constant, eternal provision from God.

The Lord shall be King over all the earth. No longer will there be many gods or divided allegiances. On that day, there will be one Lord, and His name One. Every false system of worship will be silenced.

The land around Jerusalem will be transformed—leveled out into a plain, while Jerusalem is lifted up and safely inhabited. The city will no longer experience destruction, but peace.

Those who came against Jerusalem will suffer a supernatural plague—their flesh rotting while they stand, their eyes and tongues dissolving. Panic and confusion will strike the enemies, and they'll turn on one another. God will fight for His people.

Even Judah will fight at Jerusalem, and great wealth—silver, gold, garments—will be gathered from the defeated nations.

After this judgment, survivors from all the nations that came against Jerusalem will go up year after year to worship the King, the Lord of hosts, and keep the Feast of Tabernacles. Those who refuse will face drought—no rain for Egypt, or any nation that doesn't come. Worship becomes the global norm.

Everything becomes sacred—even the bells on horses will say "HOLINESS UNTO THE LORD," and every pot in Jerusalem will be holy. There will be no more merchants or Canaanites in the house of the Lord—no more profaning of holy things.

These references are subject to interpretation, and different religious traditions may have varying views on how these prophecies apply to the end-times.

To summarize everything, because of Israel's apostasy, Israel will be attacked by every nation which surrounds it. Just when it looks like all is lost, God shows up and saves the day. As I write this, it has now been one year since Hamas attacked Israel, and they have just survived a ballistic missile attack from Iran a few days ago.

The countries that have currently attacked Israel include Lebanon (the base for Hezbollah), the Gaza Strip (the base for Hamas), and Iran. The United States and Jordan have come to Israel's aid in intercepting most of the missiles lobbed at Israel. Nevertheless, some missiles did strike military installations and civilian areas, including parts of Tel Aviv and the Negev region. [1]

According to prophecy, the attacks will continue for three and a half years before God stops them, or Jesus comes back, or both.

Our job as Christians, is to pray, pray, pray for the peace of Jerusalem.

Shalom.

---

1. The Iran Primer

Now You Know

The young people were dancing under a very large statue of Buddha. (Thou shalt have no other gods before Me.)

They came to "do" love. (Thou shalt not commit adultery [this included fornication].)

They had gotten away from God.

[God] is the same yesterday, today, and forever. Hebrews 13:8 says, *"Jesus Christ the same yesterday, and to day, and for ever."* However, Jesus and God are One. [1]

I have had people tell me, "God wouldn't do that!" See Hebrews 13:8. Reread everything God has done to Israel in the past. Therefore, isn't it conceivable that God would do the same thing again?

The Jews in Israel are returning to the synagogues, though. They are returning to God. God will relent and accept His people again.

Shalom, Israel.

---

1. John 10:30

Post Script:

On Wednesday, September 18, 2024, the United Nations General Assembly passed a resolution that effectively calls for the transfer of significant portions of Jerusalem, including the Wailing Wall, the Temple Mount, Old Jerusalem, and the Church of the Holy Sepulchre, to Palestinian control. This decision includes the Jewish and Christian Quarters and other historically and religiously significant sites such as synagogues, Solomon's Throne, the Via Dolorosa, and the tomb of Jesus.

The resolution, drafted by Palestinian authorities, who are NOT members of the United Nations, demands that the Jewish population vacate the Old City and that Judea, Samaria, and parts of eastern Jerusalem be made "Judenrein," or free of Jewish presence, within a year. The vote passed with a large majority, 124 in favor, 14 against, and 43 abstentions. The resolution aims to enforce a July advisory ruling by the International Court of Justice, which deemed Israel's presence in the areas beyond the 1949 armistice line illegal. The International Court of Justice has issued a warrant for the arrest of Netanyahu. If he steps out of Israel, he will be arrested and put in jail, facing death.

In addition, the resolution mandates the full withdrawal of the Israeli Defense Forces (IDF) from Judea, Samaria, eastern Jerusalem, and the Gaza Strip within 12 months. It also calls for a ban on arms sales to Israel that might be used in these territories and urges an international boycott of products produced by Jewish communities. Notably, the resolution does not address Israel's security concerns, the historical ties of the Jewish people to these lands, or the recent terror attacks by Hamas in Israel on October 7.

Prophetic Context and What It Means for Israel, the U.S., and Christians:

Biblical prophecy speaks of a time in the future when Israel will face an overwhelming attack from nations surrounding it. In Ezekiel 38 and 39, the Bible describes a coalition of nations coming against Israel in the Last Days. Zechariah 12:3 echoes this, warning that all nations will come against Jerusalem, but God will intervene to save His people. This is often interpreted as a sign that, despite seeming hopelessness and the destruction that may befall Israel, divine intervention will ultimately lead to Israel's deliverance.

For the United States, this has serious implications. If the U.S. were to distance itself from supporting Israel, many believe it would invite God's judgment based on the promise in Genesis 12:3, where God says He will bless those who bless Israel and curse those who curse Israel. Thus, continued support for Israel is seen as not just a political stance but a spiritual responsibility.

Scripture calls Christians to pray for Israel and stand by God's chosen people. Psalm 122:6 encourages believers to "Pray for the peace of Jerusalem," while Romans 11 reminds us that the Jewish people remain central in God's plan. Our acts toward Israel should reflect love, support, and intercession, understanding that God's covenant with Israel has eternal significance, and Christians must align themselves with His purposes.

There were 14 nations that voted against this resolution, including the United States. There were 43 abstentions, including the United Kingdom.

Furthermore, Israel was ordered to vacate all of Judea, which is the southern half of Israel, and Samaria, which is located on the western side of Israel but north of Israel's boundary. The U.S. Embassy was moved to Jerusalem during President Trump's term of office. It is where it belongs.

We, as a nation, but more so as Christians, need to pray for Jerusalem and Israel. Pray for God's protection, prophecy will be fulfilled, and Israel will triumph.

The U.N. veto power is the power of the five permanent members of the U.N. Security Council:

China

Russia

France

United Kingdom

United States

These countries have the power to veto any decision other than a "procedural" decision. If this were submitted in a meeting of the Security Council, it would only take one of the five permanent members of the U.N. Security Council to veto a resolution. The five permanent members each have veto power, meaning that if any one of them votes against a resolution, it is rejected.

However, this resolution was passed in an Emergency Special Session of the United Nations General Assembly, rather than in the U.N. Security Council, where veto power applies.

Here's the distinction:

U.N. Security Council (UNSC): The five permanent members (P5) — China, France, Russia, the U.K., and the U.S. — have veto power. In the Security Council, if any one of these countries vetoes a resolution, it fails, regardless of the support from other members.

U.N. General Assembly (UNGA): The General Assembly, where all member states are represented, does not grant veto power to any country. Votes are taken by majority, and no country can single-handedly block a resolution.

When a resolution fails in the Security Council due to a veto, the U.N. can invoke the "Uniting for Peace" resolution (General Assembly Resolution 377A), adopted in 1950 during the Korean War. This resolution allows the General Assembly to take up matters of peace and security if the Security Council is deadlocked. It provides a mechanism for an Emergency Special Session, where the General Assembly can vote on issues of international peace and security.

In such a case, even if the U.S. or another permanent member votes against the resolution, their vote does not have veto power. A simple majority vote is required for the resolution to pass. Since the Palestinians are not a member state, they do not vote but can submit proposals and participate in debates. So, in this case, the resolution passed because it was voted on in the General Assembly, where veto power does not apply. Being passed in the General Assembly and not in the security Council, also means the resolution is non-enforceable. This means that the liberals will be appeased because the resolution passed, and the conservatives will be appeased because it cannot force Israel to comply.

Other Books by the Author

Revelation: What John Knew
    Revelation: What John Knew Not
(with J. L. Hart)
(Out of Print)
War in Israel and Revelation
(First Edition)
TRUMP: Why He Lost the Election in 2020
Prophecy About Biden: Bye, Bye, Biden

(Caution: The books about Trump and Biden are exactly alike except for a personal letter to Trump in his book. There is also an additional paragraph in the Biden book that covers the prophecy concerning his presidency. (The author knows people who will never touch anything with the name Trump on it, and the same for Biden)

About the Author

Barbara Schobl-Legee
Raised in a military family from Florida, Schobl-Legee journeyed across the United States, embracing diverse faith experiences.

Baptized into the Baptist faith, she later became an ordained Pentecostal Holiness preacher and served as an Associate Pastor at Gospel Tabernacle and Antioch Southern Baptist Church.

Marrying into a Catholic family, Barbara and her husband found common ground in the Episcopal Church, where she now serves as a Licensed Lay Preacher in the Diocese of Central Florida.

Her fascination with prophecy, dating back to 2008, led her to pen four books on the subject. In promoting her prophecy books, she earned the title of international author, reaching readers in the U.K., Australia, and Canada.

Additionally, she's an international speaker and Bible teacher, sharing insights and teachings with Kenyan women via Messenger.

www.ingramcontent.com/pod-product-compliance
Lightning Source LLC
Chambersburg PA
CBHW071313040426
42444CB00009B/2008